Kerry Walsh

Read & Resp[...]

FOR KS1

Read & Respond

FOR KS1

Author: Celia Warren

Development Editor: Simret Brar

Editor: Roanne Charles

Assistant Editor: Margaret Eaton

Series Designer: Anna Oliwa

Designer: Q2A Media

Illustrations: David McKee

Designed using Adobe InDesign

Published by Scholastic Ltd, Villiers House,
Clarendon Avenue, Leamington Spa,
Warwickshire CV32 5PR

www.scholastic.co.uk

Printed by Bell & Bain

1 2 3 4 5 6 7 8 9   8 9 0 1 2 3 4 5 6 7

British Library Cataloguing-in-Publication Data
A catalogue record for this book is available from the British Library.

ISBN 978-1407-10004-3

Acknowledgements

The publishers gratefully acknowledge permission to reproduce the following copyright material: **Andersen Press** for text extracts from *Elmer* by David McKee © 1989, David McKee (1989, Andersen Press Ltd) and illustrations from *Elmer and Friends: First Colouring/Activity Book* © 2006, David McKee (2007, Andersen Press Ltd). Every effort has been made to trace copyright holders for the works reproduced in this book, and the publishers apologise for any inadvertent omissions.

Elmer

SECTION 1

About the book

Described in *Publishers Weekly* as 'a celebration of individuality and laughter', *Elmer* is a firm favourite with children. So popular is the story of the colourful elephant, that it is already considered a classic. Elmer is an immediately recognisable character, with his features on many items of merchandise as well as in a lengthy series of sequel books in which he stars. First published in 1989, the story shows young readers, through gentle humour and delightful illustration, that it is fine to be yourself and to be different from others.

The book is full of teaching opportunities: as well as discussions based on the theme of the book, children will learn colours, for example, as they enjoy the patchwork Elmer's games with plain grey elephants in the jungle. Both text and pictures offer many points of discussion and opportunities for learning, such as the names of other wild animals, and comparisons of shape, size and pattern – including the chance to hone fine discriminatory skill, which is an ideal pre-reading exercise. Many of the illustrations encourage talk that will elicit the use of comparatives and superlatives, through appropriate questions such as: *Which is the biggest/oldest/tallest elephant? Whose trunk is longer?* The story is rich in adjectives which, in turn, will extend children's vocabulary.

This book is the first of a long series about the character. Whetting children's appetites with this title will encourage them to look for and read further titles about Elmer. It is worthwhile visiting the publisher's website, www.andersenpress.co.uk, where some space is dedicated especially to Elmer. You can read a conversation between Elmer and his creator, David McKee, discover more titles and even download an Elmer colouring page – perfect for children gaining pencil control while getting to know the story's central character.

Plot summary

Elmer is different from all his friends, who are grey. He is a multicoloured patchwork elephant. He is also the life and soul of the herd, always joking and making everyone laugh. One day, he decides he no longer wants to be different. Resourcefully, he dyes himself grey with berry juice. Now none of his friends recognises him. At last, Elmer's strong sense of humour comes to the fore and he makes them all jump in surprise – and then laugh again at his joke. As the rain washes off his disguise, Elmer becomes happy to be himself. And so begins Elmer's Day – in celebration of Elmer's return and in recognition of the fun of 'dressing up' in disguise.

About the author

David McKee was born in Devon in 1935. After attending the local grammar school, he studied at Plymouth College of Art. Even before creating Elmer, David McKee's gift for illustration and storytelling appeared in books and animation, with characters such as Mr Benn, whose adventures begin when trying on costumes in a fancy dress shop. These were followed by the adventures of King Rollo – again, in books and in animated cartoons for television. Older readers will enjoy seeking out books by the same author to extend their reading experience. Most of David McKee's books are for children and published by Andersen Press.

Facts and figures
Elmer
Author: David McKee
First published: 1989 by Andersen Press Ltd
Paperback edition: Red Fox 1991

Guided reading

SECTION 2

Cover and title page

Many children may already be familiar with Elmer's image before starting school. They may have met him in the form of cuddly toys or other merchandise such as nursery feeding sets of bowls, cups and plates.

Display the cover and invite comparison between Elmer and other elephants. Elmer is camouflaged on the cover and it may take a short while for the children to discern the outline and other features, such as Elmer's ears. Encourage the children to trace Elmer's outline with a forefinger. As this is a picture book, the illustrations are as important a factor as the text. Identify the author's name and the book's title, as well as using the terms 'cover' and 'title page'. Ask the children to compare the cover text and the title page, where title and author word-order is reversed. Can they see the difference and read the words? Can they spot the publisher's logo – the little red fox?

Spread 1

The other elephants are introduced ahead of the main character. After you have read the spread to the children, point out the collective noun 'herd' and compare it with, for example, a herd of cows, flock of sheep, litter of kittens. Note the unusual syntax, where adjectives follow the noun: 'Elephants young, elephants old…'. Make the most of the rhythm of the text as you read aloud. Note how, by putting the noun before the adjectives, the focus is held on 'elephants'. Take time to compare the different elephants, made easier as they are drawn all facing the same direction. Invite the use of comparatives and superlatives. Consider the last words, 'except Elmer'. Ask if any of the elephants is a different colour. The children may suggest that one or two look blue. Talk about shades of colour and show how description can be modified – 'bluish grey', 'pinky grey'.

Spread 2

By varying the shades of grey of ordinary elephants on the previous page – described in the text as 'elephant colour' – the complete contrast of Elmer's colouring is exaggeratedly different. The patchwork patterning, in combination with the diverse bright colours, further defines his complete otherness. Talk in more detail about Elmer's pattern as well as colour, using terms such as 'checked', 'squares' and 'straight lines'. Encourage the children to note the common opening to sentences, 'Elmer was…', and to practise the colour words. Invite them to identify examples of each colour in the picture of Elmer. Also make use of counting opportunities: the birds and leaves on the tree. Discuss what the author-illustrator's use of colour (and the brightly painted sun) suggest about the climate of the story's setting.

Spread 3

Before reading the text, ask the children to describe what is happening in the picture and if they can guess the elephants' mood. Do they know any friends or family members who are like Elmer, always joking or making people laugh? Prompt the children to describe Elmer's position (upside down).

Spread 4

Read the text and draw attention to the humorous use of language: 'think a *think*', using the verb as a noun, instead of 'thought'. Discuss the difference between laughing *with* someone and laughing *at* them. Could this distinction become blurred and make Elmer suddenly wish he were not different? Ask the children to explain the meaning of 'unnoticed'. Encourage them to look closely at the elephants' different positions and attitudes that show they are on the point of waking up after their night's sleep – yawning, half-open eyes, stretching. Draw the children's attention to Elmer's backward look, and ask: *Is he wondering if any of his friends have noticed him tip-toeing away?*

Spread 5

Ask the children if they can identify the seven different animals in the picture. Which are hardest to spot? (Perhaps the giraffe?) Ask if Elmer is easy to see in this picture or on the cover. Go on to talk about camouflage and its importance to animals' safety. Ask younger children how many times they can spot the word Elmer in the text. Point out that his name, like theirs, begins with a capital letter.

Spread 6

Do the children think seeing the tree with berries gave Elmer his idea, or if the idea came to him before then? Prompt them to justify their answer, noting: '...Elmer found what he was looking for...'. What colour are the berries? What better way than just 'grey' did David McKee use to describe the berries? ('Elephant-coloured'.) Draw attention to the repetition of Elmer's action – 'shook it and shook it' – indicating that it was hard work and that Elmer was determined.

Spread 7

Read the text and look at the picture. How far through the process of dyeing himself is Elmer in the illustration? Ask the children to explain their opinions with reference to both words and picture – for example, the number of different ways he needed to roll, the quantity of unsquashed berries still on the ground, the amount of colour still visible on Elmer.

Spread 8

Compare this picture with that on Spread 5. Are the animals lined up in the same order? Are they all awake? Note the effect of the more muted colours, suggestive of evening. Ask how Elmer knows that the herd no longer recognises him. (The greeting no longer uses his name; simply 'elephant'.)

Spread 9

There is a clue in the text that helps the reader to identify Elmer even though he is now elephant-coloured. Can the children find it? ('in the *middle* of the herd'.) What visual clue is there to Elmer's identity? How does his stance and expression typify his character? (Dancing, not still; bright-eyed and watchful of others' reactions). Discuss the meaning of 'worked his way'. Why did the author not write, say, 'went', 'walked' or 'tip-toed' to the middle? Tell the children to stand up and ask one child to demonstrate 'working their way' to the middle.

Spread 10

Do the children think Elmer had been gone long from his friends? How does the text indicate that time is passing? Draw attention to the opening words 'After a while...'. Quite a time has passed by now. Encourage the children to find similar expressions earlier in the story – 'As he walked...', 'After a long walk...', 'After that...'. Why does Elmer think of the cloud as 'same old rain cloud'? Have we seen it before?

Spreads 11 and 12

After reading the text, ask the children to stand up, very still, with their arms by their sides and to adopt a very serious expression. Re-read the sibilant adjectives describing the elephants, making the most of their alliteration. How long before somebody wants to laugh? Now they know how Elmer felt! Why does the text end with an unfinished sentence?

Turn the page and enjoy the impact of the combined picture and text. Turn back to the previous spread, re-reading the text and telling the children to be ready to read together the loud 'BOO!' when you turn the page. Discuss how you know it is loud. (From the size and positioning of the word, the full capitals and exclamation mark.)

Spread 13

Enjoy counting and comparing the ten elephants' different positions as they jump in surprise. What do the elephants mean by 'It must be Elmer'? How did they work out who had made them jump? (Draw on knowledge of Elmer's character.) Compare the pink background of this picture with the green background of the first spread. Help the children to see that the bright colour reflects and emphasises the excitement and fun and break from normality in this scene.

Spread 14

Ask why Elmer's dye washes off the top of him first; why are his legs still grey in the picture? Examine the body language of the laughing elephants – one clutching his or her stomach; another pushing a third, and so on. Explain the literal and figurative meaning of the words 'show your true colours': showing our true colours helps others to see our personality, what makes us behave as we do. In Elmer's case, the berry-dye washing away also showed his literally true colours. Draw attention to the capitalisation of Elmer's Day – the phrase becoming a name, in a similar way to other special days such as New Year's Day.

Spread 15

Invite the children to choose their favourite elephant decoration, describing it in words rather than by simply pointing; using colour, shape and motif words, and stretching their active vocabulary in the process. Encourage others to listen and point to which elephant they think is being described. How does the picture suggest that Elmer's Day is a *noisy* parade? Observe how some elephants work in twos to make a sound (cooperating to play cymbals, and triangle and stick). Discuss why Elmer isn't in bright colours on this one day a year. ('Ordinary' elephant colour is special to him; it commemorates how Elmer's Day began; he is Elmer *and* he is an elephant.) Relate the climax of the story to celebrations that the children enjoy; encourage them to identify with the characters by considering how they dress up for special occasions. What is the very last word of the story? ('Elmer'.) Notice how this is a satisfying ending to the story, drawing a circle back to the title of the book.

Shared reading

SECTION 3

Extract 1

- The layout of the text – from the first pages of the book – follows the same format as in its original context. Compare the first and second paragraphs, the former with conventional layout, the latter effectively listing Elmer's colours (and, as such, a useful word-list resource). Demonstrate how this would be presented conventionally and discuss how the layout chosen is appropriate for this book.
- Invite the children to re-read sections of the extract – 'Elephants young... fat or thin', taking up the rhythm. Explain the reversed word order to focus attention on 'elephants'.
- Ask individual children in turn to read the 'and [colour]' lines as you read out the second paragraph.
- Underline the capital letters, at the beginning of sentences and of proper nouns. Highlight the common digraph, 'el', common to 'Elmer' and 'elephant'.
- Invite the children to underline specific high-frequency words, such as 'a', 'and', 'all' and 'was'.

Extract 2

- Talk about the indications that Elmer did not notice what was different straight away, including the opening time phrase, 'After a while'.
- Point out the functions of different punctuation marks, especially the use of commas (in lists), the question mark and full stops. Read the first paragraph aloud, pausing at full stops and commas and raising your voice slightly for the question, while pointing at the punctuation to highlight its effect. Note in the second paragraph how the colon separates the simple statement from the reason why it is significant.
- Highlight the adjectives in the next paragraph, establishing that they all describe the elephants. Do the children notice anything special about the choice of adjectives in the second sentence? (They all begin with 's'.) Read the sentence aloud, slowly and seriously, to show how the words emphasise this aspect of the image they create, making us want to laugh with Elmer. Can the children keep a straight face as you read?
- Draw attention to the construction of 'The more (he looked)... the more (he wanted)'. Invite the children to invent similar comparative constructions of their own, such as: 'The more I look at the pictures, the more I laugh.'

Extract 3

- Highlight the punctuation used in direct speech, especially the opening and closing speech marks and the comma or full stop inside the closing marks. Note the tag words 'gasped' and 'said'. Invite suggestions of other such words.
- The extract contains a number of long-vowel digraphs: encourage the children to identify and underline words including 'ai', (rain, again); 'ou' (cloud); 'ow' (show); 'ue' (true); 'ay' (played); 'ee' (been).
- Together, clap the rhythm of the three-syllable words 'elephant', 'celebrate' and 'decorate'. Write them on the board, breaking each word into syllables: el-e-phant, cel-e-brate, dec-or-ate. Encourage the children to learn these spellings.
- Underline the 'ed' added to the past tense verbs 'laughed', 'washed', 'gasped' and 'played'. Ask the children to pick out the stem word for each, as you cover the 'ed' ending. Re-read the full word each time as you reveal it again.
- Challenge the children to find small words within compound words: 'patch/work', 'an/other', 'him/self'.

Extract 1

There was once a herd of elephants.
Elephants young, elephants
old, elephants tall or fat or thin.
Elephants like this, that or the other, all
different but all happy and all the same
colour. All, that is, except Elmer.

Elmer was
different.
Elmer was
patchwork.
Elmer was yellow
and orange
and red
and pink
and purple
and blue
and green
and black
and white.
Elmer was *not*
elephant colour.

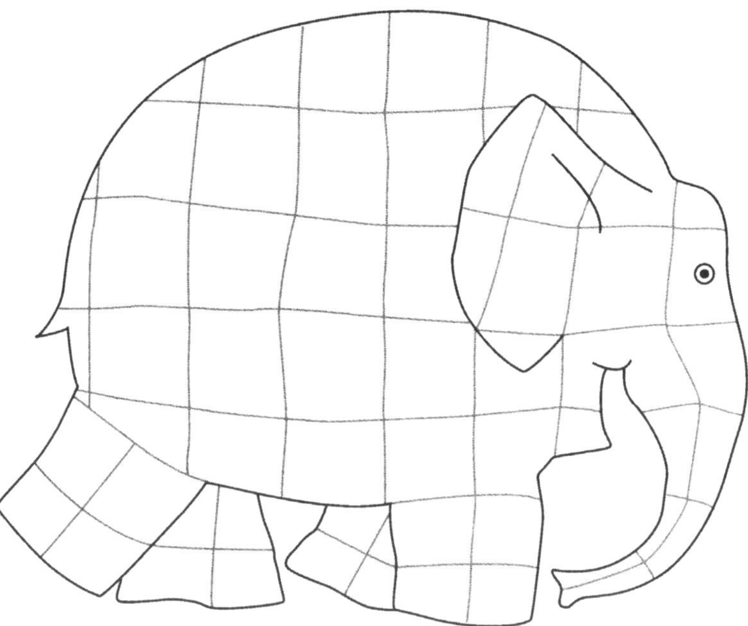

Extract 2

After a while Elmer felt that something was wrong. But what? He looked around: same old jungle, same old bright sky, same old rain cloud that came over from time to time and lastly same old elephants. Elmer looked at them.

The elephants were standing absolutely still: Elmer had never seen them so serious before. The more he looked at the serious, silent, still, standing elephants, the more he wanted to laugh.

Extract 3

As they laughed, the rain cloud burst and when the rain fell on Elmer his patchwork started to show again. The elephants still laughed as Elmer was washed back to normal. "Oh, Elmer," gasped an old elephant. "You've played some good jokes, but this has been the biggest laugh of all. It didn't take you long to show your true colours."

"We must celebrate this day every year," said another. "This will be Elmer's Day. All elephants must decorate themselves and Elmer will decorate himself elephant colour."

Plot, character and setting

SECTION 4

Whatever next?

Objective: To make predictions showing an understanding of ideas, events and characters.
What you need: Copies of *Elmer*; paper and pencils.

What to do

- This activity introduces *Elmer* to children who are new to the book. Read the first four pages aloud. Discuss the time of day that Elmer starts doubting himself. Should he have been asleep? Do people tend to worry more when they are awake at night?
- Do the children think Elmer was right to think that the other elephants were laughing *at* him? Look at the text and illustrations for clues.
- Ask them to imagine themselves as one of the elephants waking up to find Elmer gone. Would they notice straight away?
- Invite suggestions about what might happen next. Where could Elmer have gone? What might he do? Encourage the children to think broadly – might he meet another elephant like himself? Will something happen to make him change the 'think' that he's thinking?
- Turn the page to see what does happen. Is it possible to tell whether the other animals are pleased to see Elmer or are laughing at him?
- Carry on reading together, up to '...pleased that he wasn't recognised.' Again, invite the children to suggest *what next?*, based on what they know of Elmer and the other elephants.

Differentiation
For older/more confident learners: Invite the children to write down their predictions and read on by themselves to see if they are right.
For younger/less confident learners: Give textual pointers to help children to draw conclusions ('It was Elmer who kept the elephants happy' does not suggest they laughed *at* him, but *with* him.)

Patterns of language

Objective: To explore the effect of patterns of language and repeated words and phrases.
What you need: Photocopies of Extract 1 (page 8); paper; plain and coloured pencils; flashcards from an enlarged photocopy of page 15.

What to do

- Read Extract 1 with the children, asking them to underline the word 'elephants' each time.
- Demonstrate how, in normal speech, adjectives precede the noun: rephrase the second sentence as 'Young elephants, old elephants, tall or fat or thin elephants.'
- Re-read the same sentence from the extract, noting how the emphasis falls on their underlined 'elephants' words. Compare the rhythm of the phrasing and discuss its effect. (More lively; leading up to and so adding weight to 'but all happy'.)
- Point out the importance of adjectives in describing scenes/characters. Ask the children to underline each adjective in the first paragraph.
- Clarify that colours are also adjectives. In the second paragraph, point out the list layout of the colour words. Read it aloud, demonstrating how the layout forces a pause, emphasising each 'and' and building up the surprise and humour as each successive colour is added.
- Ask the children to underline each colour adjective on photocopiable page 15 with a matching coloured pencil.

Differentiation
For older/more confident learners: Challenge the children to rewrite the first paragraph of the story, substituting different adjectives.
For younger/less confident learners: Ask the children to arrange colour-word flashcards vertically in the same order as they appear in the text. Slide the 'and' flashcard down the left-hand side as they read their 'Elmer was...' list.

Plot, character and setting

SECTION 4

Thinking

Objective: To give some reasons for why things happen in a story or why characters change.
What you need: Copies of *Elmer*; photocopiable page 16; scissors; glue.

What to do

- Working in pairs, ask the children to read the text on Spreads 3 and 4. Ask: *Had anything happened to upset Elmer?* (No, he simply 'felt tired of being different'.)
- Let the pairs discuss what the elephants think of and expect of Elmer, and what he thinks and expects of them.
- Give out copies of page 16 for the children to sort the statements into the respective thought bubbles.
- Encourage them to read to the end of the story to remind themselves what happened next and gather more insights into Elmer's friendship with the other elephants.
- Bring the class together to share their opinions. Invite individuals to select quotes directly from the book to support their views.
- Do the children think Elmer is happier at the beginning or the end of the story? Is he thinking the same 'think'? Is he happy 'in his own skin'? How do we know? (The elephants were sad in his absence; they were laughing *with* not *at* Elmer; Elmer's sense of humour needed an outlet; he wanted to make them laugh again; he knows he belongs with them.)

Differentiation
For older/more confident learners: Draw two large thought bubbles for the children to write in statements of their own, instead of sorting those on the photocopiable page.
For younger/less confident learners: Arrange for an adult to read with the children and guide their discussions, relating their talk to evidence in the text.

Contrasts

Objective: To engage with books through exploration and interpretation.
Cross-curricular links: PE; drama.
What you need: Copies of *Elmer*; a tambourine.

What to do

- Explore the illustrations in the book. Suggest that Elmer not only looks different, but he behaves differently from the other elephants too. He first appears facing in the opposite direction to the herd shown on the previous page.
- Explain to the children that they are going to act out the story's contrasts of character, action and interaction.
- Establish a signal, such as holding the book above your head, for the children to stop and change, as they act out:
  - Grey elephants keeping very still.
  - In groups of six, working together to make balancing shapes.
  - Using body language to demonstrate laughter (such as rolling, rocking to and fro).
  - In groups of six, one role-playing Elmer, sadly walking off alone, the others asleep.
  - Elmer shaking the tree, then rolling in all directions until covered in juice.
- Now ask all the children to form a group (a herd of elephants), close together but not touching. Allow them to take turns to be Elmer 'working his way' into the middle of the herd.
- Ask the children to act asleep, ready to bounce in all directions on a call of 'BOO!'
- Finally, ask them to parade. Use a tambourine to provide different tempos and rhythms.

Differentiation
For older/more confident learners: Ask the children to develop facial expressions to match their actions.
For younger/less confident learners: Limit and guide the actions to very simple contrasts.

In and out of context

Objective: To use syntax and context when reading for meaning.
What you need: An enlarged photocopy of Extract 2 (page 9); felt-tipped pen.

What to do

- Read Extract 2 aloud, pointing to the start of each line for the children to follow.
- Explain that an extract is 'out of context'. Identify contextual and syntactical clues that show this does not come from a non-fiction book. For example, 'felt' (feelings belong to stories); 'But what?' (conversational tone, suited to stories); 'He looked around' (third person past tense narrative).
- Looking solely at this extract, ask: *Is there anything to indicate that Elmer is an elephant?* (There isn't.)
- How can we tell that this extract is from the middle of the story? Look at the opening phrase 'After a while', the repeated 'same old...' suggesting the reader's knowledge of the setting, the use of 'Elmer' and 'the elephants' (not 'some' elephants) showing they have already been introduced. The scene is incomplete too – Elmer wants to laugh, but he hasn't yet!
- In turn, ask individuals to underline an adjective: 'wrong', 'old', 'bright', 'still', 'serious', 'silent', 'standing' (adjectival verb). Explore how these add colour, atmosphere and detail.
- Invite suggestions for alternative adjectives to describe the elephants, such as 'grim', 'quiet', 'unmoving', 'upright'. Discuss the effect of the repeated onset letter 's' in building up the humour and tension.

Differentiation
For older/more confident learners: Challenge the children to think of adjectives to describe Elmer's state of mind and feelings, such as 'puzzled', 'amused', 'inquisitive', 'interested', 'confused'.
For younger/less confident learners: Work with a smaller group of children.

Fiction or non-fiction?

Objective: To recognise the main elements that shape different texts.
What you need: Copies of *Elmer*; information texts about elephants; photocopiable page 17; pencils; yellow and blue pencils or crayons.

What to do

- Remind the children that *Elmer* is a made-up story. Tell them that they are now going to look at non-fiction texts, with factual content.
- First, list the children's suggestions of anything in *Elmer* that is true (for example, that real elephants are grey and some live in the jungle).
- Ask the children, in groups, to find out more facts about elephants. Allow a spokesperson for each group to present their findings and show which book(s) or text(s) they came from. Add these facts to the list on the board.
- Ask the children to imagine that *Elmer* is a non-fiction book. Together create a list of humorous nonsense 'facts' about elephants to reinforce the difference between fact and fiction. This list might include: elephants have personal names; they tell jokes and play tricks on each other; one day each year elephants paint themselves pretty colours to dress up.
- Finally, hand out photocopiable page 17 for the children to sort the sentences according to whether they are from fiction or non-fiction.

Differentiation
For older/more confident learners: Help the children to combine some of their elephant facts into a non-fiction paragraph about elephants.
For younger/less confident learners: Ask an adult to read with the children and discuss each sentence.

Plot, character and setting

SECTION 4

Story elements

Objective: To identify main events and characters in stories; to find specific information in simple texts.
What you need: Copies of *Elmer*; paper and pencils; familiar stories such as 'Little Red Riding Hood' and 'Cinderella' or familiar modern fiction.

What to do

- List the following headings on the board, leaving some space under each: Setting; Key character (hero); Other main character(s); Lesser characters.
- Ask the children to help you fill the columns from *Elmer*: jungle; Elmer; other elephants; jungle animals (such as lion and giraffe).
- Organise the children into groups to discuss whether these headings apply to all stories. Appoint one child to list the group's answers under each heading. (Let them pick stories they know, or allocate a book or two to each group.)
- Give time for each group to share their responses with the whole class, and invite agreement/disagreement.
- Extend the whole-class discussion to consider if all stories have a beginning, a middle and an end. Then focus the discussion on *Elmer*. What is life like in the jungle at the beginning of the story? (All elephants are happy, being amused by Elmer.) What happens in the middle? (Elmer starts having doubts about himself and tries to change, causing concern in the herd.) How does this alter things at the end? (Elmer becomes happy to be himself; the other elephants find a way to celebrate a return to happy times and the joy of individuality.)

Differentiation
For older/more confident learners: Challenge the children to present their findings about the beginning, middle and ending of *Elmer* as a three-box-graphic abridged version of the story: a simple drawing in each box, plus one or two sentences below each picture.
For younger/less confident learners: Ask the children to draw the setting and the characters under simple headings.

Signposts

Objective: To draw together ideas and information from across a text, noting 'signposts' in the text.
What you need: Copies of *Elmer*; photocopiable page 18; pencils.

What to do

- Tell the children that they are going to explore *Elmer*, looking for signs of what happens, when and why, collecting evidence to support their findings.
- Give out copies of the book along with photocopiable page 18, enlarged. Read the words on the signposts together and explain how the responses to the first sign were arrived at. Find the evidence in the book to support the statement 'Elmer was not like other elephants.' The story says 'Elmer was patchwork.' Then identify and describe the picture – as shown in the thought bubble – that reinforces the statement. (Both from the second double-page spread.)
- Work on another signpost together, inviting the children to write their quotation and/or notes in the appropriate spaces.
- Ask the children to carry on looking for signs in the story to complete the sheet. Remind them to look carefully at both words and pictures.

Differentiation
For older/more confident learners: Challenge the children to add another signpost offering a statement regarding the character, plot or setting.
For younger/less confident learners: Write appropriate text quotations on cards for the children to match to the signposts and locate in the book.

Patterns of language

Elmer was	
yellow	and
orange	red
pink	purple
blue	green
black	white

Thinking

When Elmer goes off on his own...

- What does Elmer THINK that the other elephants are thinking?
- What DO the other elephants think of Elmer?
- What do YOU think?

I think that Elmer thinks:

I think that the other elephants think:

They are laughing at me because I am different.	He makes us happy.
I don't like being a patchwork elephant.	We like Elmer's jokes.
Elmer makes us smile. He is fun to be with.	I don't want anyone to notice or recognise me.

SCHOLASTIC
www.scholastic.co.uk

Fiction or non-fiction?

- Read the sentences below. Some come from the story of Elmer, some come from non-fiction books about elephants.
- At the end of each sentence, colour the squares:
  - yellow if it is fiction (from a story)
  - blue if it is non-fiction (from a book of facts).

yellow	blue

Sometimes he joked with the other elephants.	yellow
Elephants live in groups called herds.	
A baby elephant is called a calf.	
Whoever heard of a patchwork elephant?	
An elephant has big ears and a long trunk.	
The elephants jumped and fell all ways in surprise.	
All elephants must decorate themselves.	
Elephants can live for 70 years or more.	

- Add a sentence of your own.
- Draw a blue or yellow square at the end to show if it is fiction or non-fiction.

Signposts

- Read the signposts.
- Underneath each one, copy a sentence from the book that supports what the signpost says.
- In the bubble, describe the picture that supports what the signposts says.

Elmer was not like other elephants.

Elmer was patchwork.

Elmer was fun.

Everyone knew Elmer by name.

Elmer planned his disguise.

Talk about it

SECTION 5

What makes us laugh?

Objective: To ask and answer questions, make relevant contributions, offer suggestions and take turns.
What you need: Copies of *Elmer*; paper; writing/drawing materials.

What to do

- After reading *Elmer*, hold a class discussion on what makes us laugh. Invite the children to talk about times when they have laughed helplessly.
- Ask them who is good at making others laugh. How do they do this? Does it feel good?
- By contrast, how do the children feel if someone laughs *at* them? In pairs, let them take turns in recounting an occasion when this happened to them. How did they feel?
- To prompt ideas, offer an example to help the children to distinguish between laughing at someone's antics or jokes, and laughing at the person themselves.
- Lead on to 'learning to laugh at ourselves'. Suggest that if we can see the funny side of our mishap and not take ourselves too seriously, we feel less hurt by others' laughter.
- Return to the section of the story where Elmer is thinking negative thoughts. Then jump to where he returns to find the elephants still, serious and silent. What effect did this image have on Elmer? What motivated him to shout 'BOO!'? Did Elmer anticipate the response?

Differentiation
For older/more confident learners: Invite the children to write an account of times when they laughed at somebody and a time when somebody laughed at them, using adjectives to show how they felt.
For younger/less confident learners: Invite the children to draw a picture of something that made them laugh or of someone laughing at them. Ask them to show the picture and describe the event to a friend or to the group.

Acting elephant antics

Objective: To act out a well-known story, using voices for characters.
What you need: Copies of *Elmer*; paper and craft materials; musical instruments.
Cross-curricular links: Drama; music.

What to do

- Divide the children into groups of six to eight. Allocate sections of the story to act out: Group 1: Spreads 1–3; Group 2: Spreads 4–8; Group 3: Spreads 9–13; Group 4: Spreads 14–15.
- Tell the children to re-read their section, deciding how to perform it. They need to choose roles and plan dialogue, facial expressions or miming. Ask each child to adopt an individual voice for their part.
- Ask the children to use speech directly from the text, such as Elmer in Group 2: 'Whoever heard of a patchwork elephant?'
- Encourage each 'ordinary elephant' member of Group 3 to think up a different exclamation, to accompany one elephant's 'Oh my gosh and golly!'
- Suggest that each group begins and ends with a tableau, holding themselves quite still in role. Allow them time to experiment with positioning and expression.
- Help the children to devise a way to indicate who is playing Elmer – perhaps by wearing a colourful patchwork paper sash, hat or scarf.
- Encourage everyone to join in with the end of Group 4's enactment of Elmer's Day: dancing, clapping and/or providing percussion accompaniment.

Differentiation
For older/more confident learners: Watch all four performances in sequence, so that the whole story is seen from beginning to end.
For younger/less confident learners: Arrange for an adult to work with one group at a time.

Talk about it

SECTION 5

Dressing up

Objective: To ensure everyone contributes: allocate tasks, consider alternatives, reach agreement.
What you need: Copies of *Elmer*, paper and pencils; for older children: craft materials; for younger children: masks cut from photocopiable page 22, crayons, elastic.
Cross-curricular link: Art and design.

What to do

- Divide the class into groups of six. Explain that each group will design an elephant headdress.
- Work with the children to create a list of suitable readily available materials, such as card, fabric, glue, tape, paints, straws, string, elastic.
- Specify that their design is to be worn by themselves, so they need to consider size and how to keep the headdress in place. Their design can be a mask or be worn like a hat.
- Group members should decide who will take notes; draw sketches; ensure that everyone has a turn to speak. They could take a vote on which design they adopt.
- After discussion time, bring the class together. Ask each group's spokesperson to describe their design, explaining their decisions. For example, they might be keeping the face free to allow voices to be heard, or for easier sight or breathing. How will they keep their headdress on?
- Invite questions about design details or production method. Encourage the spokespeople to use annotated sketches in their presentations.

Differentiation
For older/more confident learners: Allow children to make their headdress, noting and reporting on the reasons for any adaptations of their original design.
For younger/less confident learners: Provide photocopies of page 22 and ask the children to decorate the mask for Elmer's Day.

Being different

Objectives: To explain their views to others in a small group; to decide how to report the group's views to the class.
What you need: Copies of *Elmer*; photocopiable page 23; pencils.

What to do

- Read the first two spreads with the children. Ask how all the elephants, including Elmer, were the same; then how they differed.
- Explain that we, too, are all individual, but also have a lot in common. Invite suggestions about how we are alike and how we differ. As well as physical differences (size, features, voice pitch and so on), ask the children to consider characteristics, personality, skills and abilities. Take each class member in turn and invite peers to say something that they like about them: *Jack has a friendly smile. Chloe has lovely ginger hair. Raj can draw well. Mo tells good elephant jokes.*
- Organise groups of five children, giving each group an enlarged copy of photocopiable page 23. Appoint a scribe for the first part of the sheet, and let individuals write one point each in the second section.
- Ask groups to decide how to report their discussions to the class. Will one person speak for the group, or will the members take turns? Will they act out an interview, with one member asking questions for the others to answer?
- Let each group present their findings to the rest of the class and answer questions at the end.

Differentiation
For older/more confident learners: Work together to develop the children's findings into a celebration of individuality and the right to be different – perhaps as a class assembly.
For younger/less confident learners: Act as scribe for the children's comments and opinions, cueing them to voice their opinions to the rest of the class.

Talk about it

SECTION 5

Describing Elmer

Objective: To respond to presentations by describing characters, repeating some highlights and commenting constructively.
What you need: Copies of *Elmer*; photocopiable page 24; pencils; thesauruses.

What to do

- After reading *Elmer* with the group, and establishing that Elmer is the central character, hand out copies of photocopiable page 24. Explain to the children that they need to decide which of the adjectives given do or do not apply to Elmer. Emphasise that they should draw on the text to support their decisions.
- Talk through the examples given on the sheet: Elmer is active and stimulates others, so the box containing 'lazy' is crossed through. The word 'cheerful' describes Elmer well. Even when he is thinking negative thoughts, he remains cheerful and doesn't brood.
- As the children use the worksheet, remind them that they will need to explain their decisions. Encourage them to scan the text and pictures for evidence.
- Bring the children together to compare findings. Ask individuals to justify their decisions, retelling or quoting parts of the story.
- Invite the children to share their own adjectives added in the blank box, and to explain which part of the story inspired their ideas.

Differentiation
For older/more confident learners: Challenge the children to use a thesaurus to find exciting adjectives to describe Elmer. Help them to put these into sentences, explaining the background incident in the story that supports their description.
For younger/less confident learners: Create word cards for the children to match with the words on the phototocopiable sheet that *do* describe Elmer (for example, 'cheerful', 'friendly', 'thoughtful', 'colourful', 'funny', 'amusing').

Retelling the tale

Objectives: To retell stories orally and in writing, ordering events using story language; to write sentences neatly and legibly; to make and use notes.
What you need: Copies of *Elmer*; small blank cards; scrap paper; pens or pencils; crayons.

What to do

- Let the children re-read the story in pairs. Ask them to note on paper the main events. Write key time/sequence words on the board to help them to organise and sequence the events, such as 'First', 'Soon', 'Then', 'Next', 'At last', 'Finally'.
- Tell the children that they will be taking turns to practise retelling the story to partners. Advise them to tick off their notes as they go, changing crayon colour each time they begin a new stage of the story. So, for example, as they introduce Elmer and his friends, they may tick their notes in red. As they move on to Elmer thinking while the others slept, they may tick in blue.
- Ask the children to transfer their notes to cue cards, starting a new card whenever there is a change in the tick colour. Tell them to number their cards and put their names on the back, in case they drop them.
- Explain that they can rephrase direct speech in their retelling; they do not have to word everything the same as in the original story.
- Finally, invite individuals to retell the story (or parts of it), using their cue cards. Encourage the use of expressive intonation and gesture.

Differentiation
For older/more confident learners: Let the children add sound effects or, with partners, introduce different character voices into the narrative.
For younger/less confident learners: Ask an adult to act as scribe and help the children to determine when they are moving on to a new part of the story.

Dressing up

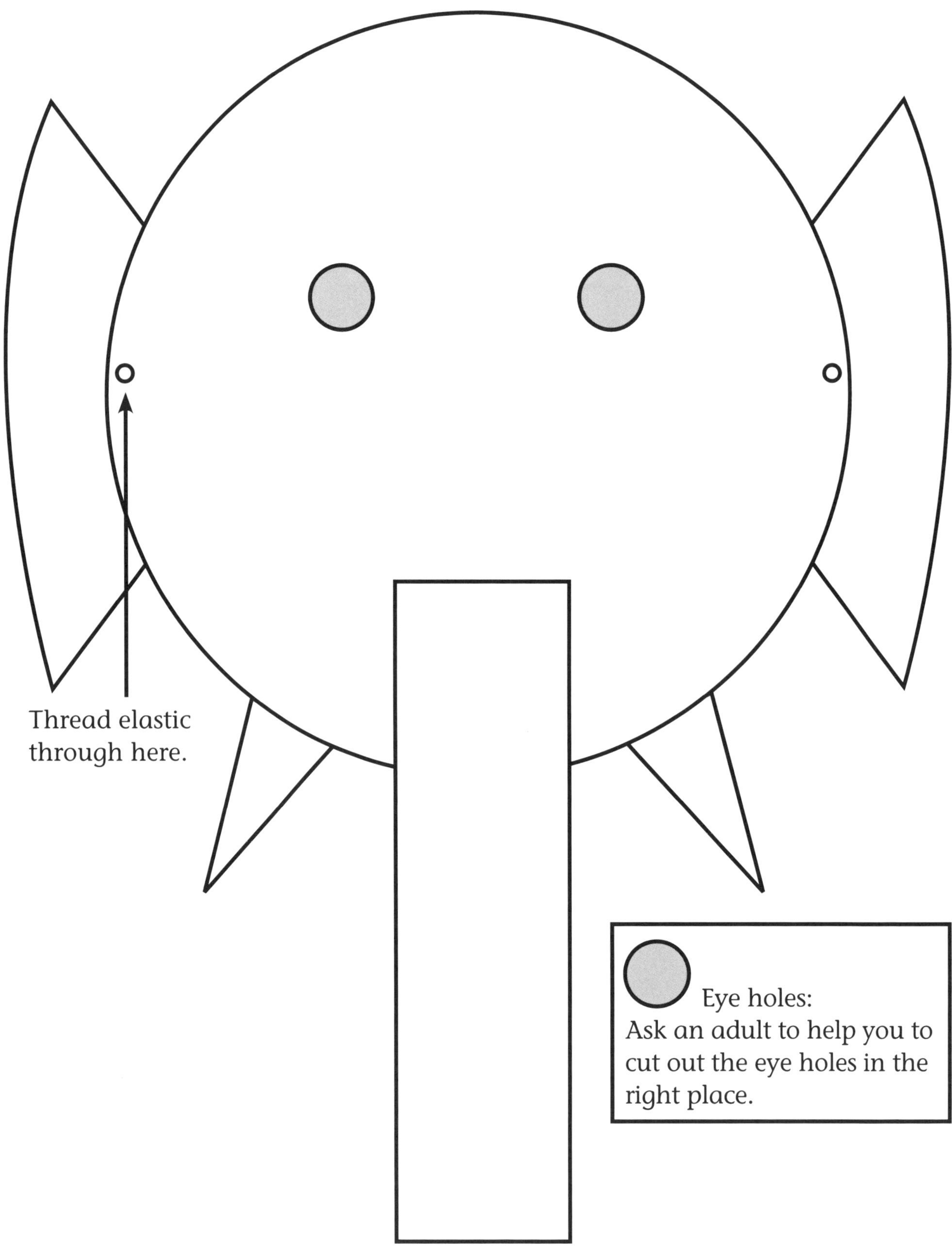
Thread elastic
through here.
Eye holes:
Ask an adult to help you to
cut out the eye holes in the
right place.

Being different

- Our group members are:

1. ______________________ 2. ______________________

3. ______________________ 4. ______________________

5. ______________________

- We think we are alike in lots of ways. These are:

- We are also different.
- Group members' comments

1. I am different because ________________ My friend says that one thing they like about me is ______________________

2. I am different because ________________ My friend says that one thing they like about me is ______________________

3. I am different because ________________ My friend says that one thing they like about me is ______________________

4. I am different because ________________ My friend says that one thing they like about me is ______________________

5. I am different because ________________ My friend says that one thing they like about me is ______________________

Describing Elmer

- Read the adjectives in the boxes.
- Colour boxes with words that describe Elmer well.
- Put a line through words that do not sound like Elmer.
- Write another word in the empty box to describe Elmer.
- Draw Elmer in the middle box.

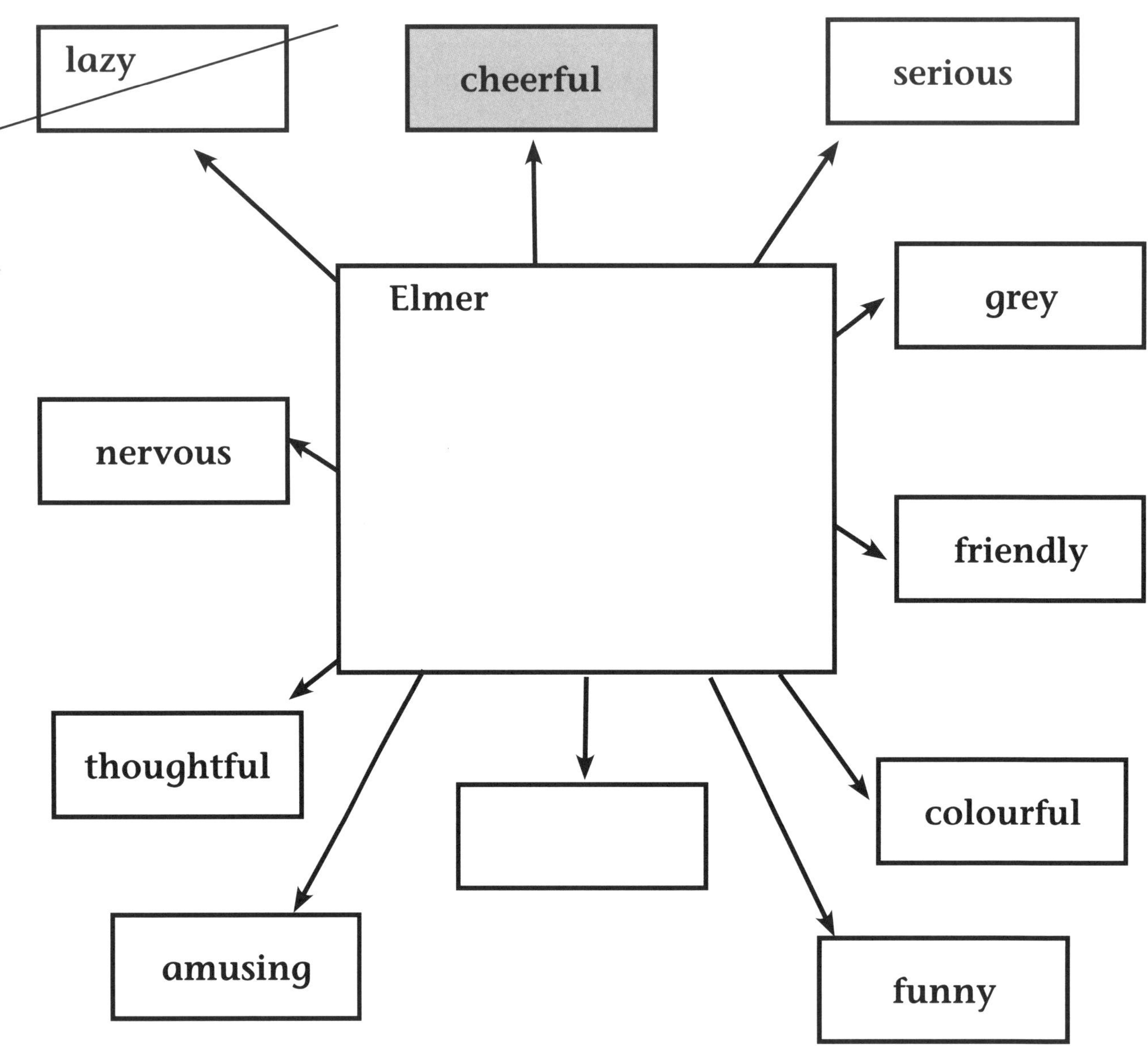

Get writing

SECTION 6

Alphabetical animals

Objective: To write legibly, using upper and lower case letters appropriately and observing correct spacing within and between words.
What you need: Copies of *Elmer*; an enlarged photocopy of Extract 1 (page 8); photocopiable page 28; pencils; highlighter pens; table-top alphabets (for younger children).

What to do

- Look at the cover of the book and ask why the author might have chosen the name Elmer for the elephant character. Point out the common initial letter and shared digraph. Can the children think of other names beginning 'El...' to create a similar effect? (Elvis, Elsie, Elaine, Elwyn and so on.) Note how some choices would change the elephant's gender.
- Display a copy of Extract 1. In contrasting colours, highlight the initial letters E/e wherever they occur in 'elephant' or 'Elmer'. Explain how the capital is used, at the onset of a proper noun and for a new sentence after a full stop.
- On Spread 5 of the book, ask the children to identify the animals. List them on the board. Draw attention to your use of lower case letters for the generic noun.
- Explain to the children that you want them to choose names for these other jungle animals, beginning with the same onset letter as their species' name. For example, there might be a frog called Fred the frog. Write this, stressing the shared initial letter and digraph, capital and lower case letters, and word spacing.
- Provide copies of photocopiable page 28. Before choosing names, the children should add the missing capital letters into the alphabet grid.

Differentiation
For older/more confident learners: Invite the children to put each animal in a sentence, such as 'Lily the lion is sunbathing.'
For younger/less confident learners: Provide individual desktop copies of the alphabet for ease of reference. Help the children to form letters correctly.

Same old same old

Objective: To write simple and compound sentences and begin to use subordination in relation to time and reason.
What you need: An enlarged copy of Extract 2 (page 9); a highlighter pen; paper and pencils.

What to do

- Read Extract 2 with the children. Highlight the repeated phrase, 'same old'. Discuss the word 'old', here indicating familiarity rather than age.
- Suggest that, when you arrived this morning, you had the 'same old thoughts'. Say: 'I walked into the classroom and looked around: same old tables, same old chairs.' Ask the children in turn to add a 'same old' item to your list. Repeat your opening line, then stop speaking and point to Child 1 who must add a phrase that begins 'Same old... (walls)'. Now point to Child 2 who must add a phrase, 'Same old... (pictures)', and so on until every child has contributed a 'same old' phrase. Offer hints by looking at items or giving an initial sound, such as *p* (for pencils).
- Challenge the children to write a sentence that begins as above. Ask them to add the same number of 'same old...' phrases as in *Elmer* (four). Remind them to write 'and lastly' before their final choice.
- Finally, ask them to add a sentence beginning 'The more I looked at the classroom, the more I wanted to...'. How will they finish it?

Differentiation
For older/more confident learners: Encourage the children to add detail to develop their sentences into a short story.
For younger/less confident learners: Provide children with a writing template to use as a cloze procedure.

Get writing

SECTION 6

Hide and seek

Objective: To sustain form in narrative, including use of person and time.
What you need: Copies of *Elmer*; paper and pencils.

What to do

- Ask the children to search the book for pictures of Elmer, noting where he is immediately identifiable, and where he is less so. Talk about how his grey disguise camouflages him.
- Discuss why the other jungle animals are less easily seen than Elmer usually is. (Their colours are not as bright; their patterns blend into the jungle background.)
- Discuss how life would be difficult for real elephants if they were coloured like Elmer. It would be hard to hide from hunters or keep their young safe. Ask: *What game do you play that would be difficult for Elmer?* (Hide and seek.)
- Invite the children to remind you how Elmer disguised himself. (Shaking down berries and rolling in the juice.) Tell them that you want them to plan a new story about Elmer and the other elephants. They are to imagine that the fictional friends want to play hide and seek in the jungle. How will Elmer find new ways to hide so that he isn't always found first?
- When the children have planned what Elmer will do, ask them to write their story, drawing on the story language and spellings from the book and including time phrases and pronouns.

Differentiation
For older/more confident learners: Encourage the children to start a new paragraph each time they move on to a fresh stage of their story.
For younger/less confident learners: Start children off with the following opening: *'Let's have a game of hide and seek,' an elephant suggested one day. 'Oh, dear,' thought Elmer, 'I shall be the first to be found, as usual.'*

Best-dressed elephant

Objective: To write simple sentences independently to communicate meaning.
What you need: Copies of *Elmer*; paper and pencils; books of art and design (for older children).

What to do

- Ask the children to look at the Elmer's Day illustration on the final page of the book. Invite individuals to describe one of the elephant's designs, talking only about patterns, shapes and colours – that is, not giving location clues such as 'at the top of the page'.
- Challenge the rest of the children to work out and point to which elephant is being described. Check with the speaker if they are right. As the children describe the elephants, list useful vocabulary, such as 'stars', 'flowers', 'striped', 'hearts', 'spotty' and so on. Older children might attempt art and cultural references (for example, modern art, Miró, Aztec), or more challenging adjectives such as 'geometric' and 'symmetrical'.
- When each elephant's costume has been described, focus on the word list. Draw attention to how the root of some adjectives is the same, such as spotty/spotted; stripy/striped).
- Ask the children to imagine they were to judge a best-dressed elephant contest. Which elephant from the illustration would they choose? Ask them to write a description of their favourite. Encourage them, after their first reference to the elephant, to use pronouns – 'he', 'she' or 'it', to refer to their chosen elephant or its design.

Differentiation
For older/more confident learners: Challenge the children to design their own elephant pattern, writing a description to accompany it.
For younger/less confident learners: Limit the children to using colour words to describe their elephant ('It is red and pink', for example), drawing a picture to match.

Get writing

SECTION 6

Let's celebrate!

Objective: To convey information and ideas in non-narrative form.
What you need: Copies of *Elmer*; writing and colouring materials; word and picture computer program; for younger children: photocopiable page 29 along with copies of Extract 1 (page 8) with colour-clue dots added beside the listed colours.
Cross-curricular links: Art and design; ITC.

What to do

- Ask the children to locate and read the book pages that describe the inception and celebration of Elmer's Day.
- Now invite them, working in pairs, to list events that they would like to see if they were elephants planning to celebrate Elmer's Day. Encourage them to take ideas from the book as well as using their imagination and experience. Their lists might include: a best-dressed elephant contest; a tug of war, a bubble-blowing game (drawing on elephants' physique); a tusk painting stall (akin to face painting or mendhi painting).
- Tell the children that, when they have planned the features of their celebration, you want them to design a poster advertising the event and its main attractions. Advise them to draft the wording before designing the layout, then think about colour, print size, use of capitals, how to use illustration, and what information to include.
- If possible, allow the children to transfer their design to computer and experiment with layout and fonts before printing. Alternatively, use traditional pencils and crayons. Challenge them to incorporate the coloured-squares patchwork design, so strongly associated with Elmer, in large box-lettering or on a balloon, for example.

Differentiation

For older/more confident learners: Ask the children to write a brief entry in an elephant's diary on Elmer's Day, as if writing after attending the event.
For younger/less confident learners: Use photocopies of page 29 for children to practise word recognition of colours.

Showing your true colours

Objective: To draw on knowledge and experience of texts in deciding and planning what and how to write.
What you need: An enlarged photocopy of Extract 3 (page 10); photocopiable page 30; pencils.

What to do

- Read Extract 3 together. Help the children to identify speech marks and speakers.
- Discuss the literal and metaphorical meaning of 'showing his true colours'. Why is this a very apt saying in this context? (Elmer's skin colours are revealed as the rain washes off the berry juice; it also reveals his practical joke, typical behaviour of the 'old' Elmer.)
- Tell the children that they are going to plan a story, in pairs or individually. Hand out copies of photocopiable page 30. Read it through with the children, discussing what the figurative expressions mean. Invite suggestions of what characters could make the sayings true, both literally and metaphorically. For example, words piped in icing sugar could be eaten; a chalk line drawn across a floor could divide a room, while figuratively creating a barrier in shared space; a scarecrow might actually lose its head.
- Challenge the children to create a character, setting and plot for a story.
- Encourage the children to use direct speech in their stories. Leave Extract 3 on display for punctuation reference.

Differentiation

For older/more confident learners: Encourage the children to construct their story in paragraphs.
For younger/less confident learners: Take suggestions for a shared group or class story, acting as scribe for the children's ideas.

Alphabetical animals

- Elmer's name begins with the same letter as **elephant**.
- His name begins with a capital letter E.

		C		E		G		I			L	
a	b	c	d	e	f	**g**	**h**	i	j	k	**l**	m
						T						Z
n	o	p	q	r	s	**t**	u	v	w	x	y	z

- Think of a name that begins with the same letter as each animal.
- Remember to begin the name with a capital letter.

Elmer the **e**lephant

T ________________ the **t**iger.

________________ the **g**iraffe.

________________ the **l**ion.

________________ the **h**ippopotamus.

________________ the **z**ebra.

________________ the **c**rocodile.

________________ the **t**ortoise.

Illustration © David McKee

- Which two animals begin with the same letter?

The ________________ and the ________________.

- Can you think of another animal that lives in the jungle?
- Give it a name.

________________ the ________________.

Let's celebrate!

- Colour the balloon to celebrate Elmer's Day.
- If there is no colour word, leave the square **white**.

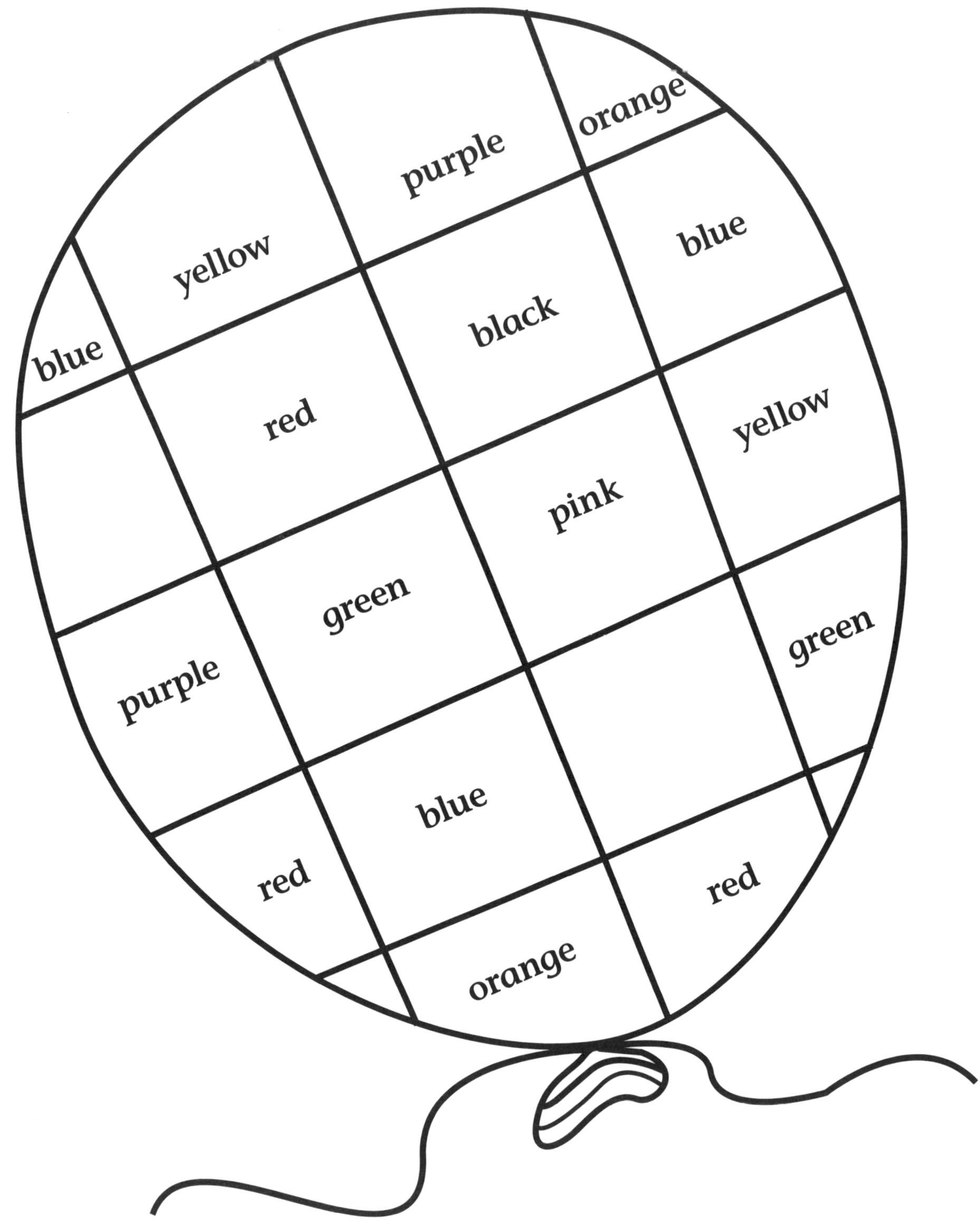

Showing your true colours

"Oh, Elmer... it didn't take you long to show your true colours."

- When someone 'shows their own colours' they reveal what they are really like. (Elmer showed his real skin colours, too!)

In the end I had to **eat my words.**

How could I really eat my own words?

- This means: I had to admit I was wrong and take back what I said.

I **draw the line** at that.

Where might I really draw a line?

- This means: I have reached the limit; I will not do anything more.

I **lost my head**.

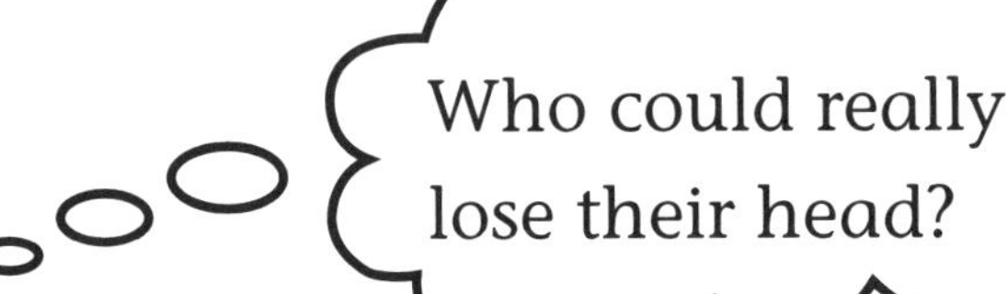

- This means: I got overexcited and went too far.

- Plan a story using a funny character. Use one of the sayings in your story.

My main character:

The saying:

How it really came true:

Assessment

SECTION 7

Assessment

Elmer is essentially a picture book. The text and pictures complement each other inseparably and need to be viewed together as a whole. The pictures illustrate the text (and for early solo readers, provide clues to the words), but they also add a kind of subtext for scrutiny and discussion. For example, the first picture of Elmer, with text devoted to introducing and describing him, also includes a delightful tree full of birds in different attitudes. Such details can be a great source of language development – 'right', 'left', 'up', 'down', 'upside down', as well as descriptions of thoughts and facial expressions. They are also an indication of the depth and humour of the book, and help to set the tone and encourage fuller, more imaginative and personal 'reading'.

Encouraging the children to talk about the pictures and the text of the story as they progress through the book will increase their intimacy with the book and develop their enjoyment of the story. Their comments will indicate their level of understanding of: the humour; thought processes (their own as well as Elmer's) and familiarity with story language; and their ability to empathise and identify with characters' behaviour and feelings.

The assessment sheet on page 32 enables children to indicate how far they have connected with the text and interpreted the story, recognising its fun way of presenting human feelings and activities, anxieties and delights, through the personification of a group of elephants.

Thinking some thinks!

Assessment focus: To visualise and comment on events, characters and ideas; to make imaginative links from a story to their own experiences.
What you need: Photocopiable page 32; pens or pencils.

What to do

- Ask the children what they think makes a good book. After sharing some ideas and examples, suggest that a good book is often one that makes you stop and think. There is a lot to think about in the story of Elmer. Give the children a few moments to recall the themes and favourite aspects.
- Tell the children that they are going to work through a sheet that asks them some questions about the book. Some of the questions will need them to read the options and choose one answer; some will require them to write an answer.
- Provide each child with a copy of photocopiable page 32. Read the title together: 'Thinking some thinks!' Ask why it says 'thinks', not 'thoughts' (using the language of the original text). This title suggests that the children will need to do some thinking themselves!
- Explain that for the earlier questions the children will need to remember what happened in the story and decide why these events happened. The last two (open) questions ask for their opinions. They should base their answers to these on what the story of Elmer has made them think about (for example, being the same; being different; being happy – or otherwise – at being themselves).
- Remind the children to read the questions carefully. Some have only one right answer. Some will have different, equally valid, answers from different children, which is why they need to *explain* some of their ideas. (Advise the children that, if they run out of space, they can turn over and write on the back of the sheet.)

Thinking some thinks!

- What was Elmer doing as he lay awake one night?

____

- Why did the other elephants not stop Elmer from going away? (tick one)

  They were eating. ☐ They were playing. ☐

  They were asleep. ☐

- Why did Elmer roll in berry juice? (tick one)

  He wanted to be different from all the other elephants. ☐

  He wanted to be the same as all the other elephants. ☐

  He wanted to be sticky all over. ☐

- What did other jungle animals say to Elmer when he was grey? (tick one)

  "Good morning, Elmer!" ☐ "Good morning, elephant!" ☐

- Explain why:__________________________________

____

- If you were an elephant living in the jungle, what would you like about Elmer?

____

____

- How does the story about Elmer make you feel about being the same as, or different from, other people?

____

____